Forty Days in the Wilderness, Wandering

poems of a Lenten quarantine

poems by

Megan Muthupandiyan

Finishing Line Press
Georgetown, Kentucky

Forty Days in the Wilderness, Wandering

poems of a Lenten quarantine

Copyright © 2021 by Megan Muthupandiyan
ISBN 978-1-64662-605-2 First Edition
All rights reserved under International and Pan-American Copyright Conventions. No part of this book may be reproduced in any manner whatsoever without written permission from the publisher, except in the case of brief quotations embodied in critical articles and reviews.

ACKNOWLEDGMENTS

Ad maiorem Dei gloriam silvarum, aquarum, desertorum, et terrarium.

Publisher: Leah Huete de Maines
Editor: Christen Kincaid
Cover Art: Megan Muthupandiyan
Cover Art: Megan Muthupandiyan
Author Photo: S. Muthupandiyan
Cover Design: Megan Muthupandiyan
Illustrations: Megan Muthupandiyan

Order online: www.finishinglinepress.com
also available on amazon.com

Author inquiries and mail orders:
Finishing Line Press
P. O. Box 1626
Georgetown, Kentucky 40324
U. S. A.

....ask yourself, dear Mr. Kappus, whether you have really lost God. Isn't it much truer to say that you have never yet possessed him?

Ranier Maria Rilke to Franz Kappus
December 23, 1903

Ash Wednesday.
26 February 2020

— The first case of infection is reported in Brazil —

You are both there and not there,
dissolving and appearing
 on the path ahead and the path within.
This heart has always been a poor cartographer
but today it seems
to be charting new shores—

like the tree bud softening its flesh
        on the grey shifts of this cloud-cast morning
I am a world within a world manifesting spring.

— Latin American countries begin contact tracing —

day two.
27 February 2020

— *New York's patient zero is hospitalized* —

We break our fast with lemon and wince
as if we have turned into a cold headwind—
the juice has seared
our parched tongues blind.

Why is bitterness so bright?
The night desert you wandered in was never lonely,
not even when the last warmth was assumed from your bones;
the stars still held your gaze with their wild shining faces,
burning with light
like the growing thousands in the crowds.

— Nigeria and the Netherlands report first cases of infection —

day three.
28 February 2020

— Global markets fall aggressively —

Wry moon—
you always seem to be in as good humor as I …
could anybody wonder why I seek out
your kinship at night?

But this evening
your slipper is ghost-worn and curling;
I quickly spin away … giddy with joy
and longing.

— California public health facilities begin receiving testing kits —

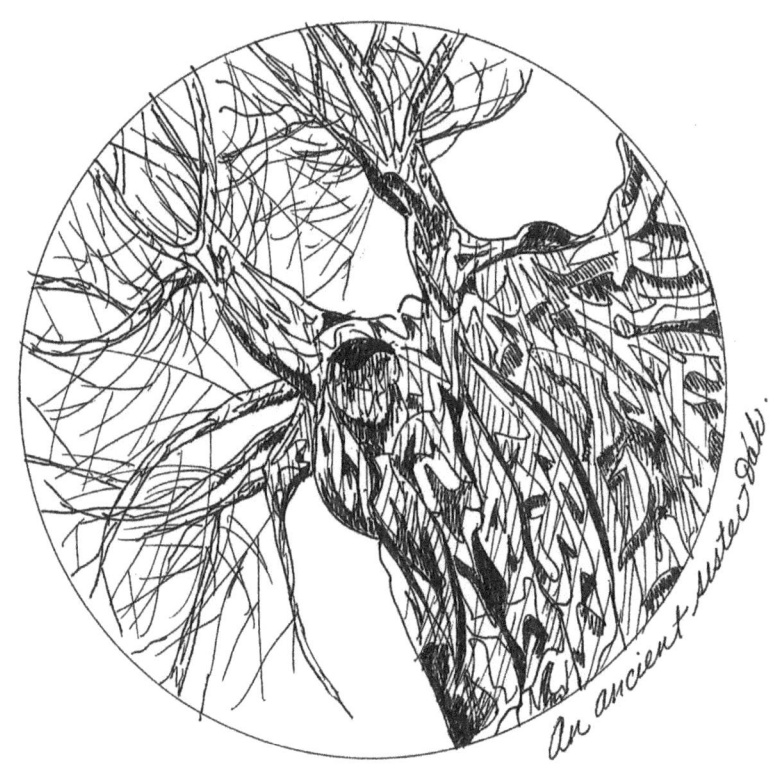

An ancient Mister Oak.

day four.
29 February 2020

— *First Coronavirus victim dies in the United States* —

There is a gift
in the death of the ash trees,
the diminishing of the village wood;
an ancient sister-oak,
massive in breadth,
can for the first time in this century
be stood beneath,
contemplated and touched.

Walk out to where it stands
alone among the stumps,
see it stalwart and strange
like a lone curiosity from
a *wunderkabinett* dismantled
at the end of a life,
an age, a fashion.

New singularity
can gild old treasure:
let your soul branch out
and take root in a wood
reduced to the thinnest groves;
rest your head
on its weathered trunk
and feel the light falling
on things of true wonder.

— Globally, eighty-thousand COVID-19 infections are confirmed —

day five.
1 March 2020

— Second COVID-19 death within the United States —

Spring announces itself
by degrees of shadow,
directing the eye
to gather
where light pools
and is denied
in the wilding of a wood
blue-branded by snow.

*— The U.S. State Department issues a Do Not Travel warning
to infection zones in Italy and South Korea —*

**day six.
2 March 2020**

— *Coronavirus death toll rises to 28 in South Korea* —

Betelgeuse burns red in
the hunter's shoulder;
it is hard
to enter another church,
gold-gilt with light—

but the altar is
adorned in spare beauty;
golden branches
rise in supplication
to the Cross
like dancers around a fire,
like seaweed buoyed
on the ocean floor,
enslaved by swells.

I kneel and think of them now,
my daughter and her father,
but if prayers come,
they are layered in images:

Orion's ancient wound
will weep forever
from holding his bow
too firm against his shoulder—

a supple dancer
will writhe like driftwood
before the flames—

eyes will water with the salty brine
of a subaltern
and restless garden—
the sway of this uncharted life.

— Indonesia reports first two cases —

day seven.
3 March 2020

— The World Health Organization reports three thousand dead globally —

Beyond the cankered limbs
of the trees
that stand at the perimeter
of his lawn
the golden disk of the sun
is poised at the horizon
pulling its devotions down.

It is late morning
where I am
when the photograph
he shares
breaks me open.

The sacred dusk
he is busy at work
witnessing
will make me feverish
with the gilt of sunset for hours;

if the memory of it
should not settle
into the shadows,
I fear I will never know
the soft dark
of my own solitude again.

— France requisitions face masks —

day eight.
4 March 2020

— *Italy closes all schools and universities* —

The elderberry bramble
may as well have
inspired
all hagiographies—

how joyously it catches
the dying light
with the curved arms of dervishes,
upraised and woven together.

and with the stout strength
of fishermen
its slowly trolls
the gold net of evening

before solemnly laying it down
with the devotion of priests
in preparation
for the day's final sacrifice.

— Iran begins using tent hospitals to address health care demands —

**day nine.
5 March 2020**

— *Lufthansa cancels over seven thousand flights* —

Drowse red-winged blackbird,
sleep after your long journey home.

I would know your call anywhere—
even if it announces you too soon.

I have opened the door in greeting
but my voice takes flight on the storm.

— Israel and Palestine place Bethlehem in lockdown —

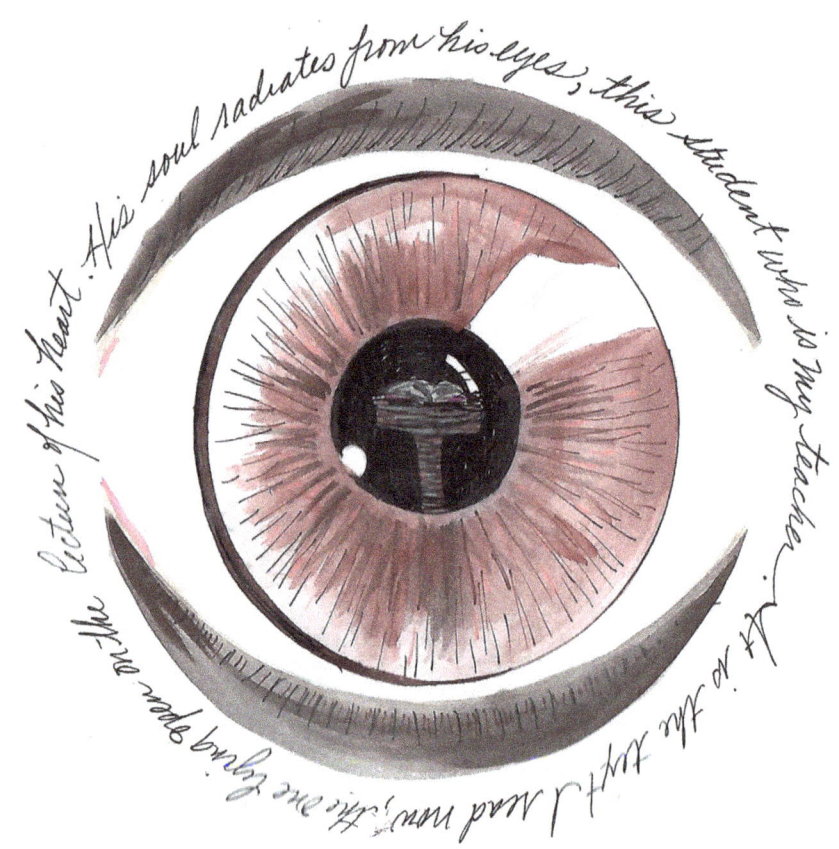

day ten.
6 March 2020

— The Czech Republic announces it will fine people $130,000 for breaking the mandatory quarantine —

For Officer Calvin Smith

His soul radiates from his eyes,
this student
who is my teacher—

it is the text I slowly read now,
the one lying open
on the sturdy lectern
of his ancient heart.

— *Iran orders nearly 60,000 mosques closed before Friday prayers* —

**day eleven.
7 March 2020**

— Saudi Arabia closes all schools and universities —

Keeping each other
like songbirds
can no longer be the fashion;

let us open our gilt cages
and watch one another fly
toward the death of certainty—
ecstatic and fearful
at having set one another free.

— Five hundred fifty cases of Coronavirus reported in the United States —

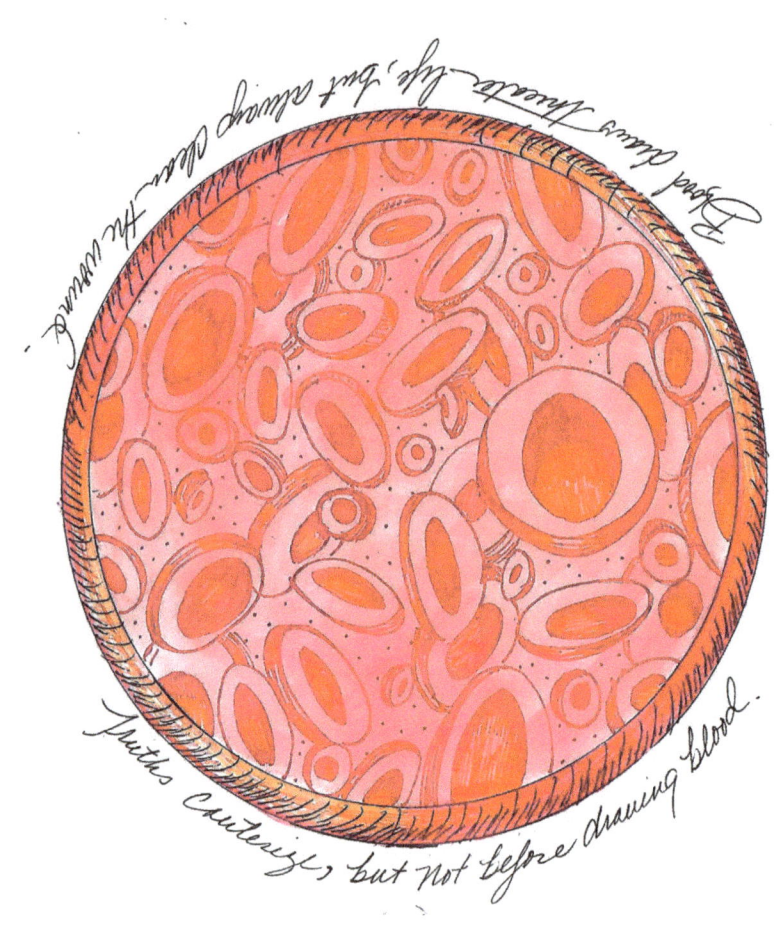

**day twelve.
8 March 2020**

— *A makeshift medical clinic in China collapses* —

Truths cauterize—
but not before drawing blood.

Blood draws threaten life,
but always clean the wound.

—Twenty-one people die in the clinic collapse —

**day thirteen.
9 March 2020**

— *Italy declares a national lockdown* —

The full moon crosses
between two limbs of a tree
as if it were only there
to be tenderly given
and graciously accepted—

the crepuscular light
of remembrance
eternally passing
between the outstretched hands
of Adam and his God.

— Iran frees seventy-thousand prisoners due to the outbreak —

day fourteen.
10 March 2020

— Turkey reports its first case —

And the quarantine begins
        as the earth softens
and the worms forget their slumber,
        as the crows gregariously gather
and the terns wheel above the pond,
        as the oak leaves turn to tissue,
and the winds choral their last song,

And the blackbirds return
        as Orion sails toward the west,
and the willow whips turn golden,
        as the carpet of clover unfolds
and the creek runs to catch the sun,
        as the dogwood blazes fiery red
and the quarantine,
        the quarantine begins.

— The Vatican closes all sites —

**day fifteen.
11 March 2020**

— The World Health Organization declares a global pandemic —

All day I felt a strange wake—
my womb
caught in wild worship
to the cloudless sky,
swaying like hands risen in praise.

And tonight it still moves
on the sight of Venus and Uranus
conjoined in the twilight;
as if it were buffering
winds wafted
by a thousand butterflies

rather than by the swell of You.

— Seven countries report their first cases —

**day sixteen.
12 March 2020**

— *The United States issues ban on flights from European Union countries* —

that stretches between two practical lives lived apart;
here and again our voices do raise, but even,
shuttered and sparkling like mica dust dancing over stone.

Striving to be as transparent as the cloudless sky
we have found a home in this arid topography
even as the harshest days scald every fiber of every leaf
and leaves them bitterly cold on the darkest nights.

                    Then again—

there are those rare, wet seasons like *that* fall or *this* spring—
when deep affection breaks through the stone
like desert blooms whose heart-roots enlarged in the darkness;
such devastating beauty they bring.

                  — Ghana reports first two cases —

**day seventeen.
13 March 2020**

— *The United States declares a federal national emergency* —

If I stop to think about what
has been lost
it isn't you
but the ash trees
that grew with roots entwined,
with lives invisible
and days invisibly numbered
until they were gone.

The sun finally made
presence of their absence—
it gave them away
the way it threw itself
in new patterns of shadow play
on the bodies of the wood,
and of the ground,
and me.

And I have mourned.

No, if I stop to think about
what has been lost,
it isn't the one
always apparent,
both ever seen and soundly present,
tattooing my body
with the light of your absence,
both when you're here
and when you're gone.

— Wisconsin closes all K-12 schools —

day eighteen.
14 March 2020

*— Georgia calls up two thousand National Guard officers
to provide medical and logistical support —*

Tonight I dreamt of him at last—
        not there—

I invited him to walk
with me to Compostela,
but he never arrived
to the place I departed . . .

        rather others began
                in his stead.

I have traveled this way
in dreams before
and know now not to wait—
        the world
does not move on
the comforts of reunion
nor the pleasures of arrivals,
but on the strange
and wonderous wanderings
of those who set out alone
and know they shall never return
this way again.

*— As COVID-19 cases in Spain jump to 4200
the nation declares a state of emergency —*

**day nineteen.
15 March 2020**

— *New York City's School System reports it will close* —

What love does in this union is dark
and difficult and glorious—
and stands on the side of life.
              —Lou Andreas Salome,
                 June 24 1914

At Compostela I stand silently
beneath the field of stars.

How do I make you understand
that love is as honest
and understated as this?

If only you had the courage
to slip into this wilderness—

You would feel it moving
slowly over you
within the satin folds of night.

— Puerto Rico issues a Stay-at-Home order —

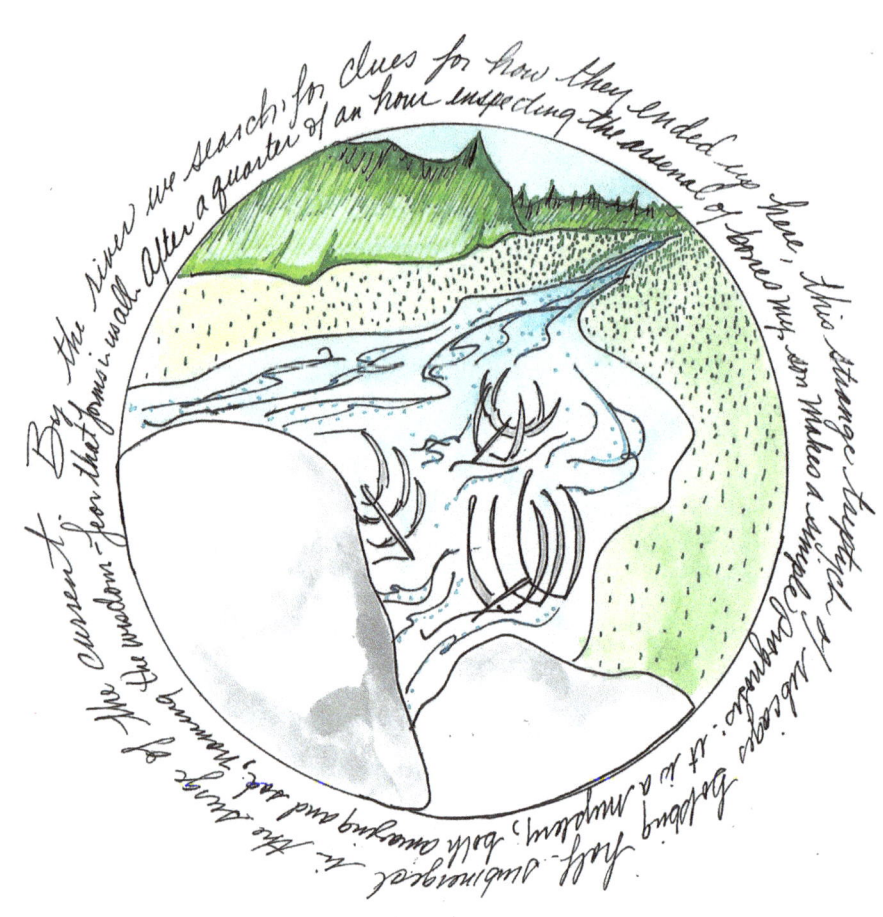

day twenty.
16 March 2020

— Columbia and Costa Rica close their borders —

By the river we search for clues
for how they ended up here,
this strange triptych of ribcages
bobbing half submersed
in the surge of the current.

After a quarter of an hour
inspecting the arsenal of bones
my son makes a simple prognosis:

it is a mystery,
both amazing and sad.

I think it is the first time
he has named for himself
the wisdom-fear
that forms in us all
in an age like this,
and it is exactly
the feeling I have.

— Ecuador and Peru implement national lockdowns —

day twenty-one.
17 March 2020

— *Venezuela begins a mandatory national quarantine* —

The little hemlock sighs incessantly
at the edge of everything,
drawing the mercuric light
into its flat-ironed scales
as if it were a tiny lizard
sunning on a rock.

Disfigured by the ice
and buried beneath the snows
the poor tree
should have died;
last winter
destroyed all harbors.

But while the towering maples
sway with the solemnity
of a Greek chorus
it lofts on the afternoon
seemingly ignorant
that nothing is expected of the flexible,
the flim-flam of the world.

— The European Union enacts a uniform travel ban —

day twenty-two.
18 March 2020

— Australia declares a human biosecurity emergency —

What does it mean to walk in faith
when our bodies become hosts
reconsecrated,
when everything we touch
bears the trace of a virus's power,
wonderful and fearfully made?

I dissolve my grief
on the tip of your tongue
before I fly
like a bright, shining arrow
through the empty aisles
of this new wilderness
thinking of the centuries
my people walked
through the stony fields
of their inheritance,
scattering mustard seeds upon the earth.

I profess, I never truly believed
in the invisible, and the unseen—
the hand of God
working in and through me,
until this moment when
touching nothing but what I will take,
I am both humbled and exalted
in the waters of skin and sweat and holy breath,
a rebaptized vector of life and death.

— Chile and Guatemala close their borders —

day twenty-three.
19 March 2020

— Forty million Californians are ordered to stay at home —

The bird congregation
is less apparent
the greater number
of trees,

but one red fox
striking out alone
through the forest
does not blend in.

— *The Bank of America suspends clients' payments* —

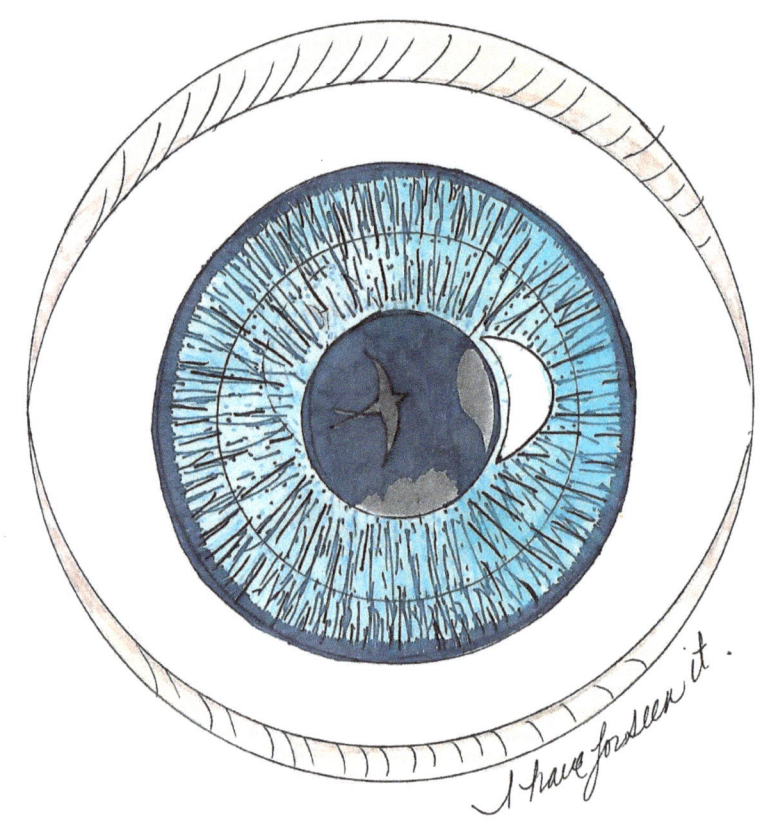

**day twenty-four.
20 March 2020**

— *General Motors commits to begin producing ventilators* —

I have foreseen it:

we will one day
watch the tree-lungs
fill with dusk,
exchange it for twilight
and exhale the dark . . .
before turning to gaze at night
surveying the cornflower fields
of one another's eyes,
coursing like swallows
in search of food.

Whether the blue-black shadows
will find what they hunt for,
I cannot foretell.

— Yosemite National Park closes —

day twenty-five.
21 March 2020

— *The United States stock market has its worst performance since the beginning of the 2008 financial crisis* —

Even before the storms
razed the forests last summer,
leaving the Northwoods
a barbed wreckage
of wood and splinter—
the white pines stood
exceptionally tall,
their limbs curling
high above the canopy.

I sought them then
as I do now,
these solitary monks
wandering a ruined world,
busy at their sacred penury,
raising their gleaming
begging bowls
to these mercuric winds,
this intemperate sun.

*— Lebanon creates checkpoints and security patrols
in communities to keep people at home —*

**day twenty-six.
22 March 2020**

— Ten thousand deaths due to COVID-19 confirmed globally —

The snow turns into rain—
        rain falls without impunity,
steel gray and galvanizing
the tender forest canopy
hanging low above our heads,
slamming into one leaf,
before sliding down
onto another,
        and another,
                and another,
and crashing into the forest floor.

Who would think
to measure
this tympanum of violence?

And what world is this,
that we can remain sheltered
in the open where others
feel its razor-wire edge
striking them,
bleeding into the frozen soil?

With whispers
of anguish or redemption,
it falls around us,
        it falls.

— Italy requests military support from the United States —

day twenty-seven.
23 March 2020

— *India grounds domestic flights* —

Attend the frogs
who sing
above your minor thoughts
in the marsh wilds—

let them overtake you
as they overtake
the wind and gull calls
before falling silent
and shimmering alive again.

— The European Space Agency reports decrease in global pollution —

**day twenty-eight.
24 March 2020**

— *The Summer 2020 Olympics postponed due to the pandemic* —

The watery reflections
of two small-leaved linden
standing at the pond's edge
touch and waver as only hearts do.

Reach me at the opposite shore,
break me apart—
a poet who enslaves the world
into image and icon.

When their lives are freed
from bondage
and restored to presence
I will be freed too.

— India declares a national lockdown —

day twenty-nine.
25 March 2020

— The United States Army appeals to retired medical personnel to re-enter service as health care workers —

Of the lake ice only shards remain,
lapping in metallic tones
on the shore.

Beneath the low wind,
the sound is otherworldly
and unmistakable:

chain mail shed in the wake
of a bloody loss
or temporary respite
before another battle, another day.

*— African finance ministers ask the International Monetary Fund
to suspend debt payments so that the countries can invest
funds into fighting the pandemic —*

day thirty.
26 March 2020

— The United States surpasses Italy with number of infections and reports one thousand deaths —

Speak out on behalf
of the left and right ventricles
of the black walnut's heart-wood,
the rich tannins of earth and leaves
at your feet—

recount your time
with the towers of violet quartzite
that bloomed
with wild meadows of lichen
beneath heavy cloud cover—

it is more than evidentiary . . .
just look around you—
this presence faces execution—

speak on its behalf.

— 3.3 million unemployment claims are filed in the United States, the highest number of initial jobless claims in the country's history —

day thirty-one.
27 March 2020

— Oil refineries in India and Europe stop production due to the sharp decrease in global demand —

How does the seed
steeped in darkness
soften and send its pith
toward the sun?

The same way
one humus-filled soul
can break another open
and make it grow.

Let me be such earth
to you;
lay your head here
and close your eyes;

my arm will take root
across your chest
as you germinate
in the growing dark.

*— Indonesia converts the 2018 Asian Games Athlete's Village
into an emergency hospital —*

The black squirrel forages

day thirty-two.
28 March 2020

— *Palestine reports its ninety-sixth case* —

The black squirrel
forages with a speed
and diligence
mistaken for skittish whim—

it is we, not he
who are moving
like dry leaves
on a misshapen wind.

— Medical professionals report reusing protective gear due to shortages —

the small wounds went unnoticed

day thirty-three.
29 March 2020

— New Orleans and Dallas convention centers declared overflow Coronavirus medical facilities —

One morning late last March
I stepped outside
and saw icicles
hanging from the Norway maple;

I walked over to inspect
and discovered that
when the sap
had begun to run
it had dripped unnoticed
from a fractured branch,
but then it froze
in an untimely frost.

For some reason
I thought about those
sweet sapsicles today
and lifted the phone to tell you
about how the small wounds
went unnoticed
until a cold spell
gave them shape;

then I put it down,
recognizing that for us
the truth in this story
is already much too late.

*— Globally, reported deaths from the virus surpass 30,000;
one third of those deaths have been reported by Italy —*

day thirty-four..
30 March 2020

— France and the United States each report over four hundred deaths in one twenty-four-hour period —

You are ill equipped
to meet my soul,
and yet the way
you have sought it . . .

had you been
better prepared
you could have
greeted it already.

*— Planes delivering medical supplies from other countries
begin arriving at JFK —*

day thirty-five.
31 March 2020

— 6.6 million unemployment claims are made by United States citizens who are out of work due to the pandemic —

When the clouds
broke open
into thin chasms of light
through the forest floor
we stood
in a slender slot canyon
carved by torrents of spring.

But we inhabited
a world half-lit,
our only footing
was an ancient deer path
that glistened steel grey
in the deep,
an ageless rivulet
still frozen,
as if from centuries before.

— *The World Bank projects that COVID-19 could propel 11 million people in developing countries into poverty* —

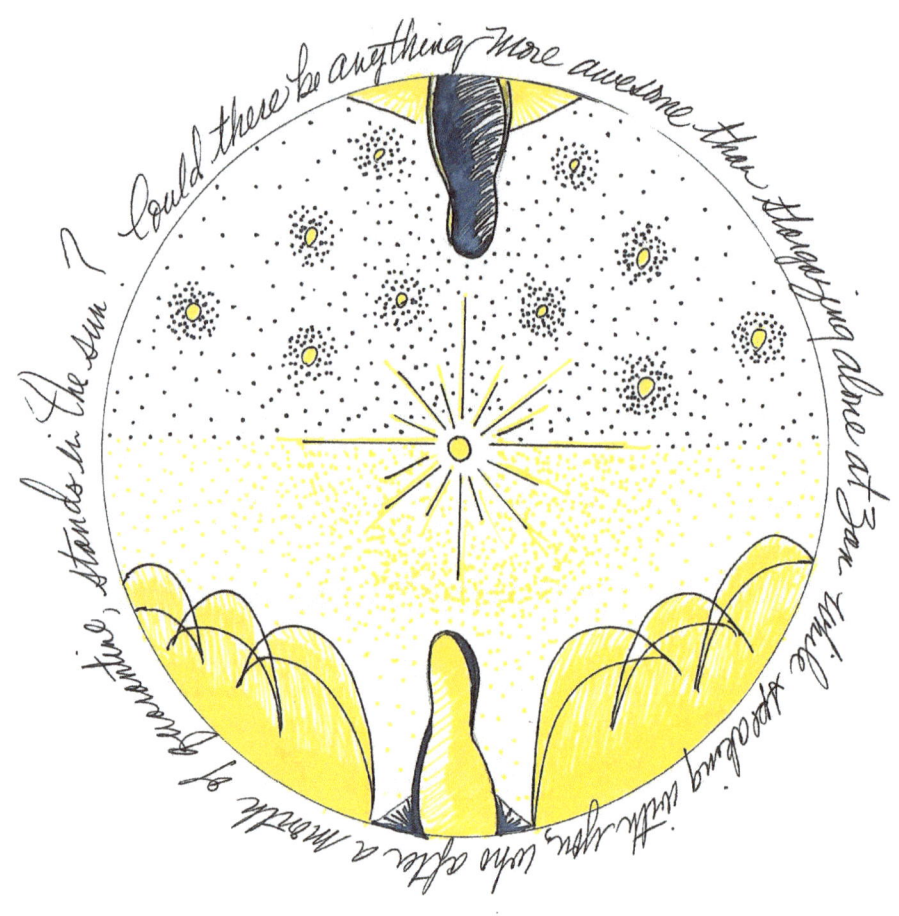

day thirty-six.
1 April 2020

— *The United Nations declares the pandemic the worst crisis the world has faced since World War Two* —

Could there be anything more awesome
than stargazing alone at three a.m.
while speaking with you,
who after a month of quarantine
stands in the sun
in the middle of a deserted
Roman street 4700 miles away?

This is the Corona Paradox:
all we have is the quotidian . . .
and yet every quotidian moment
has become more beautiful,
more sacred, somehow.

*— Across Afghanistan, scores of landlords begin a movement to waive rent
to alleviate the financial and psychological burden on their tenants —*

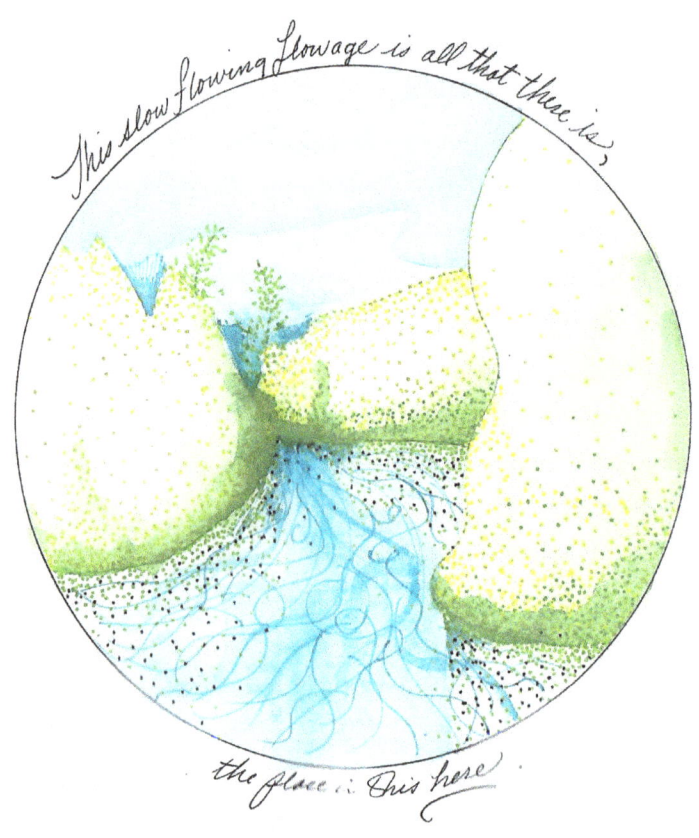

day thirty-seven.
2 April 2020

— China reports fifty percent reduction in nitrous oxide emissions due to the country's spring lockdown —

The *flowage*—

it is a name you will only find here;
a slender sink of water
gathered at the foot
of hardwood hills
that no one cared to forest,
or set the cattle in
to wander or graze.

In these parts don't ask where
the reservoir is,
or the still—
this slow flowing flowage
is all that there is,
the *place* in this *here*.

— *New York City opens a field hospital in Central Park* —

day thirty-eight.
3 April 2020

— Along the Bay of Bengal, sea turtles begin laying eggs on beaches that are no longer crowded with humans —

The spring's violence
surrendered to summer's urging,
to autumn's resignation,
to winter's resolve,
and spring has come again.

In this time of moisture uprising,
of indiscriminate killing
you ask me
what it is I need
from my friend

and I look up to the
night sky, the stars
mapping out fates and gravities
with careless predetermination,
a preconscious urge.

Set me among them—
for all I can reply
to your question is this:
to move high in the dome
of your mind
and be sought out
in clear, cold seasons
of doubt and wonder—
to be by forces
equally preordained with fate

a ritual compass
and a mysterious comfort,
an invisible and perpetual presence,
every day,
every night of your life.

*— Indian physicians treating a COVID-19 patient
are assaulted by a group of fearful onlookers —*

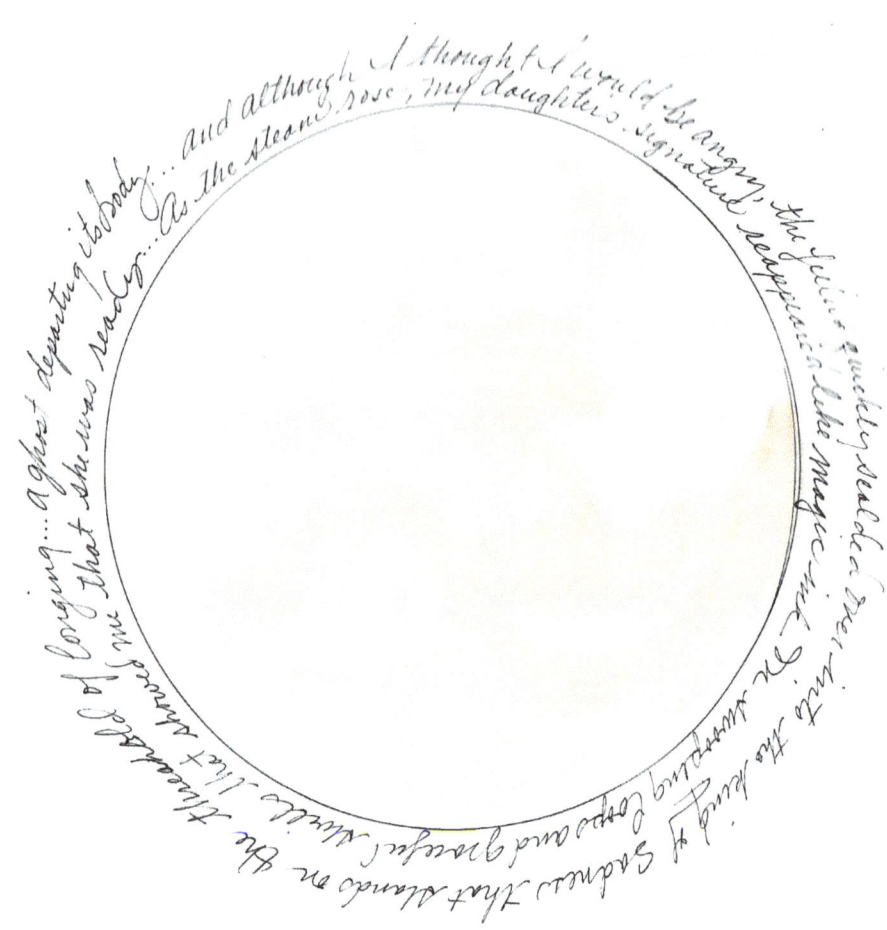

day thirty-nine.
4 April 2020

— *Projections suggest herring and other fish species will double in population through pandemic* —

As the steam rose,
my daughter's signature reappeared
like magic ink on the glass door
in swooping loops
and graceful swirls that showed me
that at least in the shower
she was ready
for the big time, baby—

and although I thought
I would be angry,
the feeling quickly scalded over
into the kind of sadness
that stands at the threshold of longing,
for just as quickly as the steam lifted,
her name dissolved in the air
like a ghost
departing from its body.

*— China commemorates the loss of its citizens to COVID-19
with a National Day of Mourning —*

The bronchioles of twilight!

day forty.
5 April 2020

— China reports zero domestic cases and thirty-four confirmed cases among people traveling from elsewhere —

The bronchioles of twilight—
tree limbs, the alveoli of buds,
draw in the blue grey evening
as if it were their last breath
before going into cave,
a deep sigh at the memory
of a feeling, a moment
that took their breath away,
and never quite gave it back.

And still the diaphragm deepens—
a violet exhalation
so blissful and devoid of mystery
that even the birds fall silent,
the reflective eyes
of the night-hunters remain closed.

The world settles like children
weaned on tenderness—
watchfully respecting
this soft communion
of anticipation,
       memory,
              breath
between the forest and its night.

— UK Prime Minister is hospitalized with COVID-19 —

day forty-one.
6 April 2020

*— Daily global carbon emissions reduce seventeen percent
due to decreased use of fossil fuel —*

At the market,
hundreds of unpurchased
Easter Lilies
herald the season
with rust brown trumpets,
that are battered at the fringe
while at the forest's edge
a single crocus has
broken through the wormwood,
a silken purse
within the uncut leather
of fallen leaves.

I hurry by both quickly,
only later wondering
how many more
of these resurrections
are left for me;
      and at last I've arrived
at a place of unknowing—
a wilderness of wasted abundance,
and fragile singularity,
one that
I shall never leave alive.

*— Over 90% of the people living in the United States
are living within a stay-at-home order —*

**day forty-two.
7 April 2020**

*— Hiring workers displaced by the pandemic,
Pakistan begins a campaign to plant ten billion trees —*

In the last moments of life
I want to remember this rising moon
pixelated by the furrows of drifting hemlocks—
to see the whole
not by circumnavigation,
but simply breaking through
the forest in an acapella of light.

And I want to carry the calls of these robins
in the conch of my ear,
to hear them hungry and feasting
on silence in the darkening forest.
greeting fellow migrants
newly returned but not yet seen,
in a voice imprinted on the heart.

And to feel alone as I do now,
as only those who love the world ever are—
wrapped in distant intimacy,
an evening communion with those others
who are witnessing and have witnessed
the miracle of time.

I have spent much of my life
seeking a place of wonder
where I can stand
warm beside another—
but before this moon
rising through the trees I can say:
I shall seek no more.

In the last moments of life
I will simply break through
like a robin's song
in the darkness,
a nameless communicant
in a larger mystery,
an acapella of light.

*—Voters in Wisconsin stand in socially distanced lines for hours
in order to vote in the state's primary —*

day forty-three.
8 April 2020

— The United States State Department reports it has repatriated 50,000 United States citizens from posts abroad —

3:14 a.m.

The rill of a solitary bird
rises above the river current
and falls—
was it from hunger or fear . . .
or just too soon?

I lean out the window
to receive the haunting desire,
the one
voiced alone in the wilderness,
and I cannot sleep—
for it is my own.

*— Demand for fossil fuel products has decreased nearly ten percent
through global lockdown —*

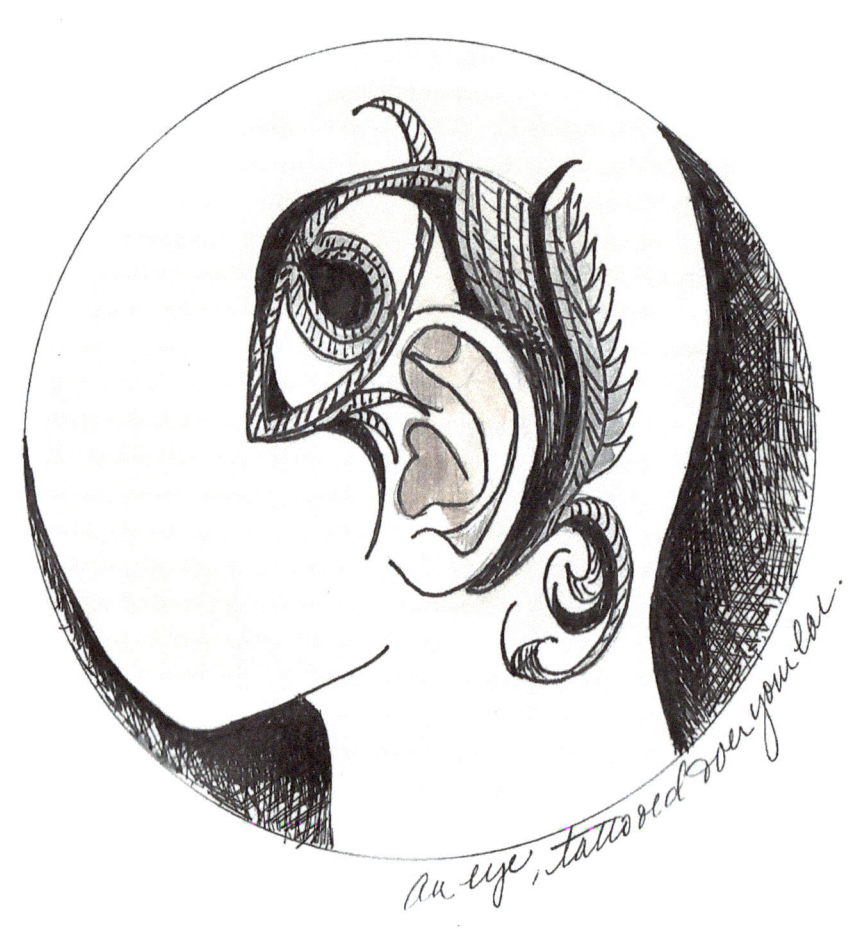

an eye, tattooed over your ear.

Holy Thursday.
9 April 2020

— *Reports of a dramatic increase in bike sales in the United States* —

You had grown your hair long,
and a beard too,
but when I teased you
that you should put it up
in a bun,
I discovered
that you only had
half a head of hair—
that the scalp was shaved
clean and tattooed,
from your ears to your neck.

And not a single tattoo,
but a host of little ones,
perhaps thirty,
commemorating important events
in your life.

I asked to take a photo
of your ink
so I could read
the biography there,
and you obliged me.

The only one I remember
seeing is an eye,
tattooed over
your left ear.

When I asked,
what about this one?
you only responded
I did it for jitterbug.

— Use of parks for recreation surges —

Good Friday.
10 April 2020

— Seismic noise during lockdown decreases fifty percent —

I dreamt that a green crane would fly near to me,
nip at my pant leg and fly away—

It did this twice, and the second time,
from somewhere far away,
I received film footage you were taking
while moving through a church—
rainbow lightning passing through the sanctuary like hail,
falling in slender strikes over and around tourists
who were moving through, unaware.

And I awoke to Jupiter burning red and low in Sagittarius,
and followed it as it rose through the tree line,
toward the waning moon, its blood red light
bleached into white as it approached,

And when it disappeared I fell back asleep
and dreamed of a small dog,
tender-footed in dancing prisms
thrown by a light catcher.

It nipped at the blazes of light, terribly scared
at the rainbow rain falling over its body,
over the places where it wanted to step,
and when I woke the dreams had been forgotten.

But when some hours later I picked up my phone
to read the poem of the day they came back:

> *Love is a rainbow that appears*
> *When heaven's sunshine lights earth's fears . . .*

I put it down and the rainbows of the night
fell over me, soaking into my skin.

Those dreams had read me as I had read the poem . . .
slowly loving me into deeper being,
as I have loved you.

— *Studies reveal the water quality of the Ganges has improved* —

Holy Saturday.
11 April 2020

*— For the first time in United States history,
every state is under a simultaneous state of emergency —*

The last light
sails over the lake
like a billowing kite—

barn swallows
nip at its tail
and lift it to the sky,
forming a strange script
while courting their shadows.

*— Canada passes a law to help employers retain employees
through the course of the pandemic —*

Easter Sunday.
12 April 2020

— During period of reduced noise pollution, birds begin singing more complex songs at a lower pitch —

purple the passion
of the tamarack bloom
when needle buds
pierce the air—
on this,
the resurrection
of spring.

— Pope Francis offers Easter Mass at a nearly empty St. Peter's Basilica; the Bishop of Canterbury leads a virtual service from his kitchen table —

Feast of St. Mark.
25 April 2020

— The number of Coronavirus-related deaths around the globe reaches two hundred thousand —

The sandhill cranes rise,
circling like ash
from the bonfires of winter
as the farmers
plait dried compost
with the soil
in long, lean braids.

When was the last time
you blessed the fields,
broke open
spare earth and stone
into something
throbbing with blood light,
woundable and wonderful?

I stand beside the fence
and watch the triptych
of creation, cultivator, land
with the silent adoration
I have received now and again
from quiet men—

I am drowning in the sensation
of silently loving,
not once wondering
if this sentiment is enough.

— Some small businesses begin opening their doors —

Third Sunday of Easter.
26 April 2020

— Twenty-eight million cases of COVID-19 have been reported worldwide —

Pursed lips break open into a sun
shot through with daggers—

in the dandelion's secret speech
I sense you have arrived.

— Furloughed Britains find new work bringing in the harvest —

Notes

The epigraph of the volume is taken from the English translation of *Rilke's Letters to a Young Poet*, translated by Stephen Mitchell.

The epigraph of "Day Nineteen" is taken from *Rilke and Andreas-Salomé: A Love Story in Letters,* translated by Edward Snow and Michael Winkler.

The poem quoted in "Good Friday" is an excerpt of Effie Waller Smith's "The Rainbow." It was published in Poem-a-Day on April 11, 2020 by The Academy of American Poets.

Acknowledgements

I am deeply grateful to the editors of the following publications for the prior publication of the following poems and illustrations:

Black Earth Institute:
    "Day Fourteen" and "Day Forty-One"

Chitro Magazine
    "And the quarantine begins" and "The arroyo wilderness"

Sheltering With Poems: Community & Connection During Covid:
    "Day Thirty-Nine" and "The Feast of Saint Mark"

Megan **Muthupandiyan** is a poet, artist, and educator. A 2019 Fellow at the Poetry Foundation's Teacher's Institute, she is passionate about creating space for people to contemplate art, poetry, and the natural world, both in and beyond the classroom. She is the founder of the Poetry in the Parks project (poetryintheparks.org), which explores the sacred beauty of land communities through short poetry films.

For more information on her illustrations and poetry visit: www.meganmuthupandiyan.com.

www.ingramcontent.com/pod-product-compliance
Lightning Source LLC
Chambersburg PA
CBHW042144160426
43201CB00022B/2407